EXPLORING CIVIL RIGHTS

THE MOVEMENT

1955

NEL YOMTOV

Franklin Watts®
An imprint of Scholastic Inc.

Content Consultants

Senator Nan Grogan Orrock
State of Georgia

Crystal R. Sanders, Ph.D.
Associate Professor of History
Pennsylvania State University

Library of Congress Cataloging-in-Publication Data
Names: Yomtov, Nelson, author.
Title: Exploring civil rights— the movement : 1955 / by Nel Yomtov.
Description: First edition. | New York : Franklin Watts, an imprint of Scholastic Inc., 2022. | Series:
   Exploring civil rights | Includes bibliographical references and index. | Audience: Ages 10–14. |
   Audience: Grades 5–8.
Identifiers: LCCN 2021020385 (print) | LCCN 2021020386 (ebook) | ISBN 9781338769715 (library
   binding) | ISBN 9781338769722 (paperback) | ISBN 9781338769739 (ebook)
Subjects: LCSH: African Americans—Civil rights—History—Juvenile literature. | Civil rights
   movements—United States—History—20th century—Juvenile literature. | Civil rights workers—
   United States—Juvenile literature. | United States—Race relations—Juvenile literature. | BISAC:
   JUVENILE NONFICTION / History / United States / 20th Century | JUVENILE NONFICTION / History /
   United States / General
Classification: LCC E185.96 .Y55 2022 (print) | LCC E185.96 (ebook) | DDC 323.1196/073—dc23
LC record available at https://lccn.loc.gov/2021020385
LC ebook record available at https://lccn.loc.gov/2021020386

10 9 8 7 6 5 4 3 2 1   22 23 24 25 26

Printed in Heshan, China 62
First edition, 2022

ON THE COVER: Black Americans sitting in the rear of a South Carolina bus, complying with segregation laws.

PREVIOUS PAGE: Mrs. Mamie Bradley, Emmett Till's mother, leaning over her son's grave at his burial.

Series produced by 22MediaWorks, Inc.
President LARY ROSENBLATT
Book design by FABIA WARGIN and AMELIA LEON
Editor SUSAN ELKIN
Copy Editor LAURIE LIEB
Fact Checker BRETTE SEMBER
Photo Researcher DAVID PAUL PRODUCTIONS

Table of Contents

Claudette Colvin, page 30

An African American bus rider stands outside a North Carolina "Colored Waiting Room" in 1940.

The Way It Was

In December 1865, the Thirteenth Amendment to the U.S. Constitution abolished slavery in the United States. By the early 1870s, former slaveholding states in the South created Black codes to strictly limit the freedom of their Black citizens. These restrictions were known as **"Jim Crow"** laws, and they controlled where people who used to be enslaved could live and work.

Jim Crow laws were expanded in the 1880s to keep Black citizens from voting or receiving a proper education. In many parts of the South, they were forced to use separate restaurants, schools, restrooms, parks, and other public places. This practice is known as **segregation**. Although laws said that these spaces should be "separate but equal," facilities for Black people were almost always inferior to those assigned to white citizens.

It was not uncommon for Black citizens in the South to be kidnapped and beaten, shot, or killed for small violations of Jim Crow laws. **Lynchings** and white mob violence frequently terrorized many Black communities. Black churches were burned down, and Black homes attacked. **Discrimination** against Black Americans also existed in the North and elsewhere in the nation, but less so than in the South at the time.

Fighting Back

Segregation, Jim Crow laws, and discrimination denied Black Americans the same **civil rights** as white Americans. In the face of **oppression** and terror, some Black Americans organized to fight inequality. The first civil rights organization in the United States was founded in 1896 as the National Association of Colored Women's Clubs. In 1909, an interracial group of **activists** formed the National Association for the Advancement of Colored People (NAACP). The NAACP called for an end to segregation in schools, public transportation, and other areas of daily life. The group also focused on making the American public aware of the violence against Black people.

In the following years, new civil rights groups emerged. Christian ministers, African American lawyers, and Black youth were especially important in organizing and supporting the emerging civil rights movement. The decade between 1955 and 1965 would serve as the heart of the movement, as action and long awaited progress began to take shape.

People stand in line to view the body of 14-year-old Emmett Till at his funeral in Chicago in 1955.

1955

This book takes a look at the most significant events in the struggle for equality during the year 1955. It examines the origins and accomplishments of important civil rights organizations such as the NAACP. It reveals how **nonviolent resistance** to unfair laws helped break down the barriers of injustice. It also visits the violent, dark side of the struggle—the murders of Black activists and innocent citizens, such as teenager Emmett Till. Lastly, it examines how Rosa Parks's segregation challenge on a Montgomery, Alabama, city bus led to a bus **boycott** there that changed the course of American history.

In the end, 1955 planted the seeds for the civil rights activism of the next decade, the most important social movement in the fight for an equal society for all Americans. ■

Opera singer Marian Anderson performed with world-famous orchestras at major concert halls throughout Europe and the United States.

1

Barriers Begin to Fall

On January 7, 1955, Marian Anderson became the first African American soloist invited to sing at the Metropolitan Opera in New York City, America's most highly respected opera house. Anderson sang the role of a fortune-teller in an Italian opera. The 57-year-old singer's historic performance was a major step in the entrance of Black performers into classical music. Before this, Black artists had mainly performed for Black audiences, while beginning to attract younger, white audiences interested in jazz and early rock 'n' roll. Few Black singers were popular among older white Americans. Anderson paved the way for other great Black opera stars such as Robert McFerrin, Leontyne Price, and Jessye Norman.

One Step Forward

Sixteen years earlier, Anderson had been barred from performing at Constitution Hall in Washington, DC, because of the color of her skin. Constitution Hall was owned by an organization called the Daughters of the American Revolution.

As a young girl, Grammy Award–winning opera singer Jessye Norman was inspired by the career of Marian Anderson.

Marian Anderson singing at the Lincoln Memorial in 1939.

When First Lady Eleanor Roosevelt learned that the owners would not permit Anderson to sing because she was Black, Roosevelt quit the organization. She arranged for another performance by Anderson at a different Washington site. On April 9, 1939, Anderson stood on the steps of the Lincoln Memorial, the nation's monument to Abraham Lincoln. In 1863, President Lincoln had issued the Emancipation Proclamation, a turning point in the government's attempt to end slavery in those states that had seceded from the Union. There, Anderson performed for a crowd of 75,000 people and millions of radio listeners.

A Black family leaves Florida for the North during the Great Migration. Many Black Americans encountered discrimination and segregation in their new northern homes.

The Great Migration

The Great Migration was the largest mass movement of people in American history. Between about 1910 and the early 1970s, more than 6 million African Americans relocated from rural regions in the South to the cities of the North, Midwest, and West. Though segregation was not legal in the North, racism and anti-Black discrimination still existed. Southern Black citizens headed north in search of better jobs, safer environments, and the basic rights denied to them in the South. The development of a thriving urban Black culture launched an era of political activism among African Americans. These important developments would lead to the civil rights breakthroughs of the 1950s and 1960s

Government Action

On January 18, 1955, President Dwight D. Eisenhower issued Executive Order 10590, which established the President's Committee on Government Employment Policy (PCGEP). An executive order is a directive from the president that has much of the same power as a **federal**, or national, law. The committee was given the task of preventing discrimination on the basis of race, color, or religion in all areas of employment for the federal government.

Though its power was limited, the PCGEP represented a step forward in the long journey to make nondiscrimination an important part of national policy.

The U.S. military remained segregated until 1948. Here an integrated unit sees action during the Korean War in 1950.

Read's drugstores were the first site of the sit-in campaign in Baltimore, Maryland.

Sitting-In for Change

The Read's drugstore chain in Baltimore had a strict policy of racial segregation at its lunch counters. At that time, many stores also had restaurants inside—long counters with stools where customers could order ice cream, sandwiches, and other lunch items. African Americans were allowed to shop at Read's, but were prohibited from being served food at the lunch counters. An activist group called the Congress of Racial Equality (CORE), formed in 1942, decided to stage a **sit-in** protesting this discriminatory policy. A sit-in is a protest in which demonstrators occupy a place, refusing to leave until their demands are met. CORE had already conducted successful campaigns to integrate private facilities. In the 1940s and early 1950s, the group used nonviolent demonstrations to integrate restaurants and businesses in Chicago, St. Louis, Boston, Washington, DC, and other major cities. Students from nearby Morgan State College, a historically Black university, joined members of CORE in an attempt to **integrate** the drugstore.

On January 20, 1955, CORE members and Morgan State students walked into Read's flagship store on Howard and Lexington Streets to stage a sit-in. The Black students sat down at the lunch counter to order food. As expected, the students were refused service, but this time they decided to stay. The sit-in lasted 20 minutes before the protesters left peacefully.

Inspired by earlier protests, Black youths stage a sit-in to desegregate the lunch counter at Katz Drug Store in Oklahoma City, Oklahoma.

At the same time, other groups of Morgan State students demonstrated at several Read's stores in nearby neighborhoods.

An official from Read's called Morgan State and asked the school to call off the students. The stores were losing money because of the protests. Many people avoided shopping at Read's because they feared violence might erupt during the sit-ins. The school and the protesters refused to back down. Within days, Read's announced it would **desegregate** its lunch counters.

The demonstrations at Read's were a turning point in the budding civil rights movement, sparking successful sit-ins elsewhere in the months and years to come. ▪

Students at a sit-in at a lunch counter in Arkansas quietly do their homework while they are refused service by restaurant staff.

An International Disgrace

Black Americans were not alone facing the challenges of segregation. The country of South Africa had a system of legal segregation known as **apartheid**. On February 9, 1955, 2,000 armed police officers forcibly relocated 60,000 Black residents of Sophiatown to a town called Meadowlands. People's homes and property were destroyed. The South African government feared its Black citizens were beginning to live too close to white areas and wanted them moved. The Meadowlands houses had no toilets, water, or electricity. Many Black Americans felt there was little difference between the system of laws legalizing apartheid in South Africa and the Jim Crow laws in the United States.

FREEDOM...
DOES NOT INCLUDE
SEGREGATION

PRESIDEN

CIVIL RIGHTS
IS RIGHT!

REGIO

MISS

CALIF

African Americans from across the United States gather to protest segregation in California.

2

Nonviolent Resistance

Young African Americans were often those citizens who challenged segregation laws with **civil disobedience**. Using this form of nonviolent protest, a person would deliberately break a law and accept the punishment, even if it meant being beaten or arrested, without fighting back. Despite the risk, it was a way to gain publicity for the injustices of segregation and to push for lawful change.

Strength through Organization

As more individuals began to challenge segregation laws, the NAACP's influence began to grow. By the mid-1950s, it was the most powerful civil rights organization in the United States. In 1954, the group appointed Medgar Evers the first state field secretary of the NAACP in Mississippi.

By 1955, his activism made him the most influential civil rights leader in the state. Evers had served in the army during World War II and later became an activist. Working with the NAACP, Evers organized voter registration drives, nonviolent protests, and boycotts of white-owned companies that practiced discrimination. He also encouraged African American students to join the NAACP. Thanks to his efforts, student-centered chapters of the organization sprouted in Black college towns such as Jackson, Hattiesburg, and Tougaloo.

NAACP civil rights leader Medgar Evers in Jackson, Mississippi, in August 1955.

Teenage Activist

Barbara Johns

The sit-ins and other nonviolent protests of 1955 were a continuation of anti-segregation protests in the South that had begun a few years earlier. In 1951, 16-year-old Barbara Johns led her classmates in a strike to protest substandard conditions at her all-Black Virginia high school. The school facilities were poor, the school equipment was outdated, and there were no science labs.

The students and the NAACP filed a lawsuit that was eventually resolved in the Supreme Court's 1954 *Brown v. Board of Education of Topeka* decision, outlawing public school segregation. In 2020, officials announced that a statue of Barbara Johns would be installed in the U.S. Capitol. It would replace one of Robert E. Lee, military leader of the proslavery Confederacy.

The Virginia Civil Rights Memorial in Richmond, Virginia, honors the courage of teenage activist Barbara Johns.

IT SEEMED LIKE REACHING FOR THE MOON.

BARBARA JOHNS

Martin Luther King, Jr., third from left, listens to a speaker at Morehouse College in Atlanta, Georgia.

Rising Star in the Civil Rights Movement

Nonviolent resistance was critical to the success of the civil rights movement. Most African Americans realized that violent protests would anger and **alienate** white people, even those who supported the civil rights movement. The push for equal rights required a leader who would embrace the beliefs of civil disobedience. In 1955, the Reverend Dr. Martin Luther King, Jr., emerged as such a leader. King strongly believed in the principle of nonviolent social change.

Dr. King served as pastor of the Dexter Avenue Baptist Church in Montgomery, Alabama, from 1954 to 1959. He then became co-pastor at Atlanta's Ebenezer Baptist Church.

The King family. Top, left to right: mother Alberta Williams King, father Martin Luther King, Sr., and grandmother Jennie Williams. Bottom, left to right: brother Alfred Daniel, sister Christine, and Martin Luther King, Jr.

King was born in Atlanta, Georgia, in 1929. His grandfather and father served as pastors of the Ebenezer Baptist Church in Atlanta. King attended segregated schools in Georgia and graduated in 1948 from Morehouse College, a distinguished historically Black men's school. He then attended Pennsylvania's Crozer Theological Seminary, where he earned a graduate degree. In 1954, King became pastor of the Dexter Avenue Baptist Church in Montgomery, Alabama. By this time, he was a member of the executive committee of the Montgomery NAACP.

King was inspired by the nonviolent teachings of Indian activist Mohandas Gandhi.

Martin Luther King, Jr., and Coretta Scott on their wedding day, June 18, 1953.

Using nonviolent resistance, Gandhi had helped India win independence from Great Britain in 1947. King first learned about Gandhi's concept of using nonviolent protests as a political tactic while he was a student at Crozer. He read everything he could find about Gandhi, including essays written by the Indian leader as well as his autobiography.

Like Gandhi, King set out to oppose injustice and inequality without resorting to violence. He would find a way to put his beliefs to use when he became involved in the historic Montgomery bus boycott of 1955 and 1956. ■

Dr. Martin Luther King, Jr., who was just a young man when Mohandas Gandhi died, considered the Indian leader his "guiding light" of nonviolent social change.

Mohandas Gandhi (center) and supporters march in India to protest the British government's tax on salt in 1930.

Nonviolent Freedom Fighter

Mohandas Gandhi was born in 1869 in Porbandar, India. After briefly attending Samaldas College, he spent three years studying law at the University of London. In 1893, he took a job with a law firm in South Africa, which was a colony of Great Britain at the time. There, he was outraged by the racial discrimination faced by Indian immigrants at the hands of white British authorities. The following year, Gandhi formed the Natal Indian Congress to fight inequality. He soon began developing and teaching the concept of nonviolent resistance to combat discrimination.

Returning to India in 1915, Gandhi led campaigns of civil disobedience, including boycotts of British schools and manufacturers and marches against discriminatory laws. Though arrested several times, Gandhi fought for the British withdrawal from India. In August 1947, India finally became an independent nation. The following year Gandhi was shot and killed by a political opponent. To this day, Gandhi is recognized worldwide as an inspiration for the movements against racism and violence.

COLORED
WAITING
ROOM

E. J. Thornton, a professor at Fisk University, and his family enter the "Colored Waiting Room" at a bus terminal in Mobile, Alabama.

3

A Challenging Spring

In addition to segregated restaurants and schools, most southern cities had a segregated bus system. In Montgomery, Alabama, Black citizens were allowed to use the same buses as white citizens, but had to follow strict rules.

Black riders were not permitted to sit in the first 10 seats in the front of the bus. These were for white riders only. African Americans were assigned the 10 seats in the back of the bus. In between the two sections were 16 seats. Anyone could sit in this middle section, but Black passengers were required to give up their seat if a white passenger boarded and the first 10 seats were occupied. Black riders were also expected to pay their fare at the front of the bus and then walk back outside to board through the rear door.

Challenging the Rules

On March 2, 1955, high school junior Claudette Colvin boarded a Montgomery City Lines bus. She was riding home on a seat in the middle section. As the bus continued along its route and picked up more passengers, every seat became occupied. The driver, Robert W. Cleere, told four Black women, including Colvin, to give up their seats to the white riders who were now standing in the aisle.

Three of the four Black riders surrendered their seats. Colvin refused. Cleere became enraged and called for the police to deal with the teen. When the officers arrived, they ordered Colvin to get up.

Claudette Colvin, 1952

In Atlanta, Georgia, in 1956, public transportation was still segregated despite the Supreme Court ruling earlier that year declaring it **unconstitutional**.

When she refused, they grabbed her wrists and dragged her off the bus. Colvin was forced into a police car, handcuffed, and taken to jail. She was charged with assault, disorderly conduct, and violating Montgomery's segregation laws. Colvin remained in jail until her pastor bailed her out hours later.

News of the arrest spread quickly through Montgomery's African American community. Lawyers from the NAACP believed Colvin's arrest could be the ideal legal test case to challenge Montgomery's segregation laws: Colvin was an excellent student, well mannered, intelligent, and deeply religious. She had also been active in the NAACP Youth Council.

The NAACP began to make plans to boycott Montgomery buses and launch a legal case against Montgomery City Lines. The plans were paused, however, when NAACP activists learned Colvin was pregnant and unmarried. Leaders were afraid the public would look on her without sympathy because of this. In the end, Colvin paid a small fine for the assault charge and returned to school.

Claudette Colvin in 1998. The day she was arrested was still clear in her mind 43 years later.

The father of sisters Linda and Terry Lynn Brown (pictured) brought a suit against the Board of Education of Topeka, Kansas, resulting in the Supreme Court decision that made segregated public education illegal.

History-Changing Legislation

While ordinary citizens were beginning to confront segregation laws in their everyday lives, other challenges were being fought in the courts. In 1954, the Supreme Court case *Brown v. Board of Education of Topeka* ruled that racial segregation of children in public schools was unconstitutional. It was the most influential and powerful ruling against the legalized separation of the races.

WE WANT EQUAL BUT SEGREGATION

KEEP CITY SCHOOL WHITE

Anti-integration protests were common throughout the South. In 1955, white teenagers march on Baltimore's city hall to protest school integration.

Southern state **legislatures** fought back against the *Brown* decision by creating laws to preserve segregation. A sweeping movement called "massive resistance" began to grow among residents of southern states in order to oppose school integration. Laws were passed to deny state funds to schools that attempted to desegregate. Many cities and counties established "whites only" private schools, using public funds to support these segregated facilities.

On April 5, 1955, Mississippi passed a law penalizing white students with jail and fines for attending school with Black students. In Tennessee, laws were passed to create separate washrooms in coal mines, where many Black men worked, and separate buildings for Black and white patients in mental institutions.

34

Brown II

In response to the South's defiance, the Supreme Court issued *Brown II* on May 31, 1955. This decision declared that local communities should move toward full observance of *Brown v. Board of Education of Topeka* "with all deliberate speed." The ruling was vague, however, and did not establish any timeline. Nor did it set a punishment for any locality that continued to defy *Brown*. ▪

Black and white schoolgirls stand together in an integrated classroom in Washington, DC, circa 1955.

John Mercer Langston

In 1855, 100 years earlier, a Black American made history in the fight for civil rights in Ohio. John Mercer Langston was born free in Louisa, Virginia, on December 14, 1829. His father was a white plantation owner and his mother a free Native American–Black woman. After his parents died, Langston was raised by a family friend who planned to move to Missouri, then a slave state. Because his guardian feared for Langston's freedom if he relocated there, the 10-year-old boy was allowed to stay in Ohio, where he was raised by Richard Long, an **abolitionist**. Long helped educate Langston about the anti-slavery movement. He later attended Oberlin College in Ohio. He then wanted to study law but was denied admittance to two law schools because of his skin color. Langston found two local abolitionists and studied the law under their guidance. It was later confirmed by a district court that his knowledge of the law enabled him to practice in Ohio.

Langston became involved in state politics, working to secure voting rights for Black men and encouraging them to seek higher education. On April 22, 1855, he became one of the first Black Americans elected to public office in the United States as the town clerk in Brownhelm Township, Ohio. Langston also served in the U.S. House of Representatives from Virginia from 1890 to 1891.

In 1869, John Mercer Langston became the first dean of the newly created law school at Howard University.

More than 50,000 people came to view Emmett Till's body and pay respect to his memory.

Summer Ends in Tragedy

Early summer witnessed a string of incidents that were sparked by the *Brown* and *Brown II* Supreme Court decisions. Several events played out on the education front, demonstrating the tense division between the opponents of segregation and of desegregation.

Breakthroughs . . . and Resistance

On June 6, Oklahoma leaders voted to admit Black students to all of the state's public colleges, including the University of Oklahoma. Two days later, on June 8, the school board of the city of Poteau became the first in Oklahoma to vote for desegregation. On June 21, the Tulsa board of education agreed to integrate its schools.

Yet resistance continued. In Virginia, on June 23, Governor Thomas Stanley proclaimed that the state would continue to segregate its schools. Stanley had at first urged Virginians to accept the *Brown* ruling, but pressure from the state's anti-integration politicians forced him to change his position.

On June 29, a federal judge ruled that African Americans could not be refused admission to the University of Alabama because of their race or color. The NAACP brought the case on behalf of student Autherine Lucy. A hostile mob had tried to prevent Lucy from attending classes at the university. When the school president's home was stoned, the university suspended Lucy for her own protection.

Autherine Lucy in 1955. More than 33 years after being expelled from the University of Alabama, Lucy enrolled again and earned a master's degree in education.

University of Alabama students protest the enrollment of Black student Autherine Lucy at the school.

Lucy sued to overturn the suspension, but the administration **expelled** her. It claimed her lawsuit had tarnished the reputation of the university.

Politicians in Georgia also took a hard stand against *Brown*. On July 11, the state board of education ordered that any teacher supporting desegregation was to be fired. Weeks later, on August 1, the board fired all Black teachers who were members of the NAACP. As a result, many of Georgia's NAACP leaders made coded membership rolls to protect their members from racist firings.

509
NO SMOKING
COLORED SEAT FROM REAR

COLLINS AVE.
TO HOLLYWOOD

Jim Crow laws reached into every corner of the South. A sign on the front of a bus in Miami, Florida, instructs African Americans to "seat from rear."

Desegregating a City's Bus System

While some civil rights activists targeted voting rights and education, the plan to desegregate public transportation was taking shape. In June 1954, Sarah Mae Flemming took the seat of a white woman who was exiting a segregated bus in Columbia, South Carolina. The driver demanded she get up from the seat. Flemming became embarrassed and got off at the next stop, two miles from her destination.

The South Carolina NAACP filed suit on Flemming's behalf in federal court, claiming her civil rights had been violated. In February 1955, the court dismissed the case. Refusing to back down, the NAACP Legal Defense and Education Fund then filed an appeal in federal court. On July 14, the court ruled that segregation on Columbia buses was illegal, an important decision in breaking down barriers in the state. However, for Black people in many other towns in the South, riding public transportation was a constant reminder they did not share the same rights as white people.

Sarah Mae Flemming's lawsuit in South Carolina helped pave the way for the eventual desegregation of buses throughout the nation.

Disneyland Opens

On July 17, 1955, Disneyland opened in Anaheim, California. The amusement park was not segregated, but it was built outside a city that had a large African American population. The park was difficult to reach by public transportation. Not many Black people living there had cars of their own. While they were welcome at Disneyland, few had any way to get there. In other areas of the country, however, theme parks were often segregated.

Emmett Till

August 28, 1955, marked one of the darkest events in civil rights history. On that day, 14-year-old Emmett Till was murdered in Money, Mississippi. Till had come from his home in Chicago to visit his great-uncle, Moses Wright, and his family. Money was a rural town with a small population and a few stores, including Bryant's Grocery & Meat Market. Most Black and white people in Money were poor and had little education.

Emmett Till with his mother, Mamie Bradley.

Bryant's Grocery & Meat Market in Money, Mississippi. The building was still standing in 2020. It is part of the Mississippi Freedom Trail. A historical marker telling the story of the Till murder stands at the spot.

Jim Crow laws ruled Mississippi. African Americans were expected to call white men and women "Mister" or "Ma'am." "Colored only" and "white only" signs were posted at restrooms, drinking fountains, bus and train station waiting rooms, and other places. Raised in the city of Chicago, young Emmett Till was unaccustomed to following the racial rules placed on Black men in the South.

On the night of Wednesday, August 24, Till and several other Black youths went to Bryant's market to buy some candy. Outside the store, Till pulled a photograph of a white girl from his wallet that he claimed he had dated. His friends dared Till to enter the market and speak to the white female clerk. Till accepted the dare and walked into Bryant's store. Roy Bryant, who was out of town on business, owned the store. His wife, Carolyn, was working the store alone. Her sister-in-law, Juanita Milam, was in an apartment in the back of the store.

Carolyn Bryant claimed Till grabbed her by the waist and asked her for a date, using inappropriate language. Till may have whistled at her, something he sometimes did to overcome a stutter in his speech. Watching from outside, Till's friends realized he had crossed the line in his behavior toward the white woman. They rushed inside to pull him out of the store. The Black youths hopped into their car and drove away.

Carolyn Bryant, wife of Roy Bryant, was at the center of the Till case.

A Shocking Crime

Carolyn Bryant and Juanita Milam agreed not to tell their husbands about the incident, fearing they would seek revenge. But Carolyn told others and the story spread. When Roy Bryant returned from his business trip, he learned what had happened. Furious, he went to the home of Till's great-uncle with J. W. Milam, Juanita's husband, at 2 a.m. on Saturday, August 28. The two men grabbed Till from his bed and forced him into their car.

Till was never seen alive again. His body was found in the Tallahatchie River three days later. The men had beaten Till, shot him in the head, and thrown his body into the river.

Roy Bryant (left) and J. W. Milam (center) sit with their attorney at their trial.

The Aftermath

Till's body was sent back to Chicago for burial. Tens of thousands of people attended the funeral. Photographs of his beaten corpse were printed in magazines and newspapers across the country.

Roy Bryant and J. W. Milam were charged with Till's murder. Reporters from around the world descended on Mississippi to cover the trial. The media sharply criticized the Jim Crow South and Mississippians themselves for their harsh treatment of African Americans. Many white southerners resented the attacks and rallied behind the defendants. Many angry southerners accused the NAACP and outsiders from the North of trying to destroy the "Southern Way of Life."

At the trial, the jury of white men acquitted Bryant and Milam. Americans were outraged by the decision. Rallies were launched across the country to protest the verdict. Dr. King was among those who most bitterly criticized the trial. Months later, Bryant and Milam confessed to murdering Till. The two men were never convicted of the crime, and Carolyn Bryant admitted that she had lied about what happened in the store with Emmett Till.

Violence Continues

Weeks after the Till murder, on October 22, another young Black man, 16-year-old John Earl Reese, was shot in a café in Gregg County, Texas. Two white men drove by the café and opened fire with a rifle. Though the shooter was convicted of murder, he received a five-year suspended sentence and was released from police custody. The charge of murder against his partner was dropped. Both men went free. ■

Reopening the Case

In 2004, the U.S. Department of Justice reopened the Emmett Till case to determine if Carolyn Bryant was guilty of playing a part in the teen's murder. The case was reopened because of renewed interest in the murder, including documentary films and new information obtained by the Justice Department. Till's body was **exhumed** and examined. A grand jury found no evidence to charge Bryant. In 2017, the Federal Bureau of Investigation reopened the case for a second time because of Bryant's confession about fabricating what transpired between her and Emmett Till. Once again, no evidence was found to charge Carolyn Bryant for any participation in Till's murder.

Roy and Carolyn Bryant sit with their two sons, Roy Jr. and Lamar, at the Till murder trial in Sumner, Mississippi. Roy Bryant died in 1994. His codefendant, J. W. Milam, died in 1980. Neither man served a day in jail for the slaying of Emmett Till.

Rosa Parks with Dr. King, circa 1955. Parks was awarded the Congressional Gold Medal in 1999, the highest civilian award in the United States.

5

An Unlikely Heroine

Media coverage of the anti-Black violence and unfair Jim Crow policies in the South captured worldwide attention. White Americans could no longer ignore the racism and discrimination suffered by African Americans.

Governmental Change

On November 7, 1955, the federal government banned racial segregation on trains and buses in interstate travel. The same day, the Supreme Court outlawed racial segregation in public parks, playgrounds, and golf courses. In both decisions, the federal government struck down the concept of "separate but equal" facilities for white and Black people.

A young Rosa McCauley (Parks) sometime between 1920 and 1930.

Who Was Rosa Parks?

Segregation on buses in most southern cities and towns continued to be a harsh reality for African Americans. That finally began to change on December 1, 1955, when Rosa Parks, a 42-year-old African American seamstress riding a bus in Montgomery, Alabama, refused to give up her seat to a white man. Parks's courageous act is considered the **catalyst** that launched the American civil rights movement.

Rosa Louise McCauley Parks was born in Tuskegee, Alabama, in 1913. Her father, James McCauley, was a skilled carpenter and stonemason. Her mother, Leona Edwards, was a teacher in Black church schools. Rosa lived with her mother, brother, and grandparents in Pine Level, Alabama, just outside the state capital, Montgomery. Parks was a deeply religious woman and a devoted member of the African Methodist Episcopal (AME) Church.

A postcard shows Rosa Parks's birthplace in Tuskegee, Alabama.

Raymond and Rosa Parks. The couple was married for 45 years, until Raymond's death in 1977. They had no children.

After graduating from her segregated high school, Parks briefly attended the Alabama State Teachers College for Negroes to become a professional educator. She gave up her studies, however, after her grandmother became ill and needed Rosa's care.

In 1932, Rosa married Raymond Parks, who became a member of the Montgomery chapter of the NAACP in 1934. Raymond encouraged Rosa to complete her degree, which she earned in 1934. She became a tailor's assistant and took sewing jobs on the side to supplement her husband's income as a barber.

In 1941, Rosa got a job at Maxwell Field, an Army Air Corps base in Montgomery. The base was integrated, but the public bus to and from Maxwell was not. Riding home on the segregated bus every day, Parks was reminded of her status as a second-class American. She joined the NAACP in December 1943 and vowed to help end the "humiliation" she and other Black bus riders felt.

Among her projects as local NAACP secretary was to organize a voter registration drive and develop plans to desegregate Montgomery city buses. Parks worked with E. D. Nixon, the executive secretary of the Montgomery chapter of the NAACP.

As a result of her cooperation with the Montgomery bus boycott, Rosa and her husband, Raymond, lost their jobs and struggled financially for years.

An Emerging Force

E. D. Nixon

By 1947, E. D. Nixon had become state president of the NAACP. As Nixon's role expanded, so did Parks's. She began doing field research, interviewing African Americans who had complained of discrimination. She attended NAACP leadership-training programs and spoke at NAACP conventions.

Officials at the NAACP headquarters in New York City discuss a poster promoting racial equality.

Parks was named secretary of the statewide NAACP. In 1949, she began work with the NAACP Youth Council, which focused on desegregation campaigns in Montgomery. These jobs were volunteer positions. At the time, Parks's paying jobs included working at a tailor shop and at the Montgomery Fair Department Store.

This photo taken in the 1950s shows Dexter Avenue in Montgomery, Alabama.

This picture was taken on December 21, 1956, the day after the U.S. Supreme Court ruled Montgomery's segregated bus system was illegal. It re-creates the event of one year earlier when Parks refused to move from her seat.

The Arrest

Shortly after 5 p.m. on December 1, 1955, a weary Rosa Parks left her job at the department store and walked to her bus stop to wait for her bus home. Bus 2857 pulled up. Parks dropped her dime in the box and stepped aboard. She took an aisle seat in the mixed middle section, behind the "Colored" sign. A Black man sat next to her. Across the aisle were two Black women. There were several empty seats in the whites-only section. The bus made several stops, picking up enough white passengers to fill the empty seats. One white man remained standing.

The bus driver turned around and locked eyes on Parks. The driver was James Blake—coincidentally, a driver who had kicked Parks off his bus 12 years earlier for the same reason. Blake motioned to Parks and the other Black passengers sitting in her row to move. They all got up. Parks slid over to the man's seat and gazed out the window.

Blake again ordered Parks to move. "No," she said. "Well, I'm going to have you arrested," he threatened. Calmly, she stared into the driver's angry face and said, "You may do that."

The police report dated December 1, 1955, says that Rosa Parks was "sitting in the white section of the bus, and would not move back."

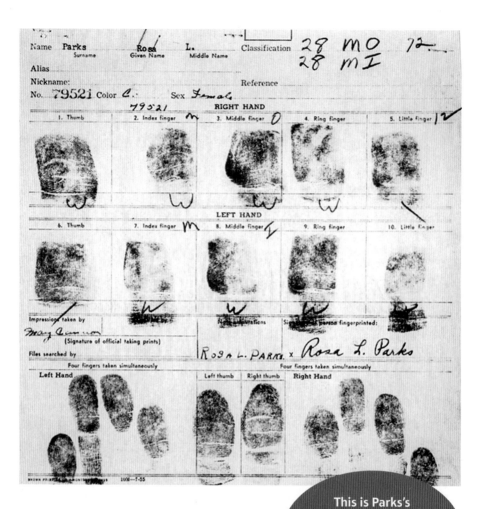

This is Parks's fingerprint card with her signature "Rosa L. Parks" seen above the box labeled "Right Hand."

Blake called the police. When officers arrived, they boarded the bus and took Parks into custody. She was taken to city hall, where she was formally arrested for disobeying segregation laws. Bail was set at $100. She was then taken to the city jail, fingerprinted, and placed in a cell. Allowed one phone call, she telephoned her husband, Raymond.

"Tired of Giving In"

News of Parks's arrest spread quickly throughout Montgomery. Within a few hours, Raymond and E. D. Nixon were heading to the city jail to bail her out. Afterward, they drove to the Parks home, where they discussed using Rosa's arrest as a test case to challenge segregation in the courts.

This image shows Parks with E. D. Nixon (center) and her lawyer, Fred Gray (right).

"It won't be easy," Nixon said. "We might have to take it all the way to the Supreme Court—and that'll be a struggle." In those brief moments, Rosa considered how a court case would affect her husband and her mother, who were both in poor health. As the family's main wage earner, could she risk their security? In the end, Rosa's belief that oppressed people had to fight back won her over. She agreed to challenge the bus segregation law. Years later, she said her decision to challenge Jim Crow was largely inspired by the murder of Emmett Till. Parks would write in her autobiography, "People always say that I didn't give up my seat because I was tired, but that isn't true . . . No, the only tired I was, was tired of giving in." ■

A group of African Americans, including Rosa Parks (standing in dark coat and hat), wait at a bus stop in Montgomery. The picture was taken on December 26, 1956, six days after the Supreme Court ruled that the city's segregated bus policy was illegal.

The Rise of R&B

The development of Black rhythm and blues (R&B) music has its roots in the Great Migration of the 20th century. By the 1950s, African American recording artists in large urban communities were tapping into traditional forms of Black-created music, such as blues and gospel, to fashion a new form of music called R&B. The year 1955 alone produced two classic R&B tunes. On May 21, Chuck Berry recorded "Maybellene," and on September 14, Little Richard recorded "Tutti Frutti."

By the 1960s, R&B songwriters had embraced the politics of the civil rights movement. Songs such as "A Change Is Gonna Come" by Sam Cooke focused on civil rights issues and found great commercial success with

This photo of an empty Montgomery City Lines bus was taken three weeks after the start of the bus boycott. The signs separating the bus into "White" and "Negro" sections have been removed.

6

A Boycott for Change

On the evening of Thursday, December 1, Fred Gray, Rosa Parks's attorney, called Jo Ann Robinson, president of the Women's Political Council, to tell her Parks had been arrested.

Getting Started

"I think we ought to call a boycott," Robinson said. Nixon and Gray agreed. Using economic pressure to bring about change in the system made sense: Montgomery City Lines needed Black riders to earn profits—more than 75 percent of all city riders were African Americans.

Robinson, an English professor at Alabama State College in Montgomery, immediately swung into action. In the early morning hours of Friday, December 2, she headed to the college.

Jo Ann Robinson

With the help of two female students and another professor, Robinson put together a flyer calling for a boycott of the city buses by Black riders for Monday, December 5. The team used the college's copying machine to run off about 35,000 copies. By 7 a.m., the flyers were ready and activists began circulating several thousand to Montgomery's African American homes, churches, schools, restaurants, and shops.

Boycotters helped Robinson and her team spread the news about the protest. This newspaper article describes how handwritten posters motivated people to join the cause.

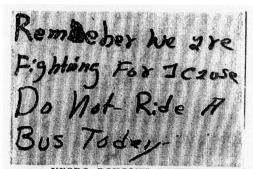

Remember we are Fighting For 1 cause Do Not Ride A Bus Today—

NEGRO BOYCOTT POSTER

This is one of the posters which city policemen yesterday removed from bus stop posts as Negroes staged a boycott against the Montgomery City Lines over arrest of a Negro woman on a transportation segregation charge. The poster states: "Remember we are fighting for a cause. Do not ride a bus today."

Several thousand Negroes use the buses on a normal day.

Police cars and motorcycles followed the buses periodically to prevent trouble after Sellers said some Negroes reported they were threatened with violence if they rode buses yesterday.

The circulars distributed in Negro residential districts Saturday urging the boycott yesterday in protest to the arrest of Rosa Parks were not signed. The Rev. A. W. Wilson, pastor of the Negro church where the meeting was to be held, said he would not disclose "under any circumstances" the names of those who asked permission to use the church for the meeting.

Ministers of various churches led the meeting last night.

Earlier, Bagley had issued a statement saying the bus company "is sorry if anyone expects us to be exempt from any state or city law."

In the Rosa Parks case yesterday, the city was prepared to offer testimony from 11 witnesses. Only three, Blake and two women passengers testified. One of the women said there was an empty seat where Rosa Parks could have sat if she had moved to the rear.

As the boycott started yesterday morning, Negroes stood on downtown street corners waiting for rides or piled into taxicabs. Many walked two or three miles to work in the crisp cold weather.

Most Negro children walked to school and there was a relay auto pickup system operating throughout most of the day.

Nixon believed the city's African American ministers could rally support for the boycott. He first recruited Ralph Abernathy, the young pastor of the First Baptist Church, the oldest and largest Black Baptist church in Montgomery. Nixon called Dr. King and convinced him to join the cause as well.

That night, more than 50 Black community leaders filled the basement of King's Dexter Avenue Baptist Church. Not everyone, however, supported the idea of a boycott. Many feared it would result in even more trouble for Montgomery's Black residents. At one point in the meeting, Rosa Parks rose from her seat to speak.

Leaders of the Montgomery bus boycott hold a meeting at the First Baptist Church in February 1956. The Reverend Ralph Abernathy (center) speaks to a packed gathering of boycotters.

Parks called for unity to challenge Jim Crow bus laws and the bus arrests of African Americans. After hearing her words, most of those in the crowd promised to support the one-day protest. Many Black ministers agreed to endorse the boycott in their Sunday sermons the next day. Throughout the weekend, local ministers met with the NAACP and the Women's Political Council to plan for the Monday morning boycott.

Churches and religious leaders played a key role in the boycott's success. Here Black residents of Montgomery listen to a speaker at a church rally to support the boycott.

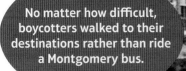

No matter how difficult, boycotters walked to their destinations rather than ride a Montgomery bus.

The Big Day

Monday, December 5, 1955, was cold, windy, and rainy in Montgomery, less than ideal conditions for the boycott. Yet hardly a Black rider could be found on a city bus that day. Nearly 100 percent of Black residents who used Montgomery City Lines buses participated in the boycott. Some 40,000 boycotters walked to their destinations, while others traveled in car pools, on bicycles, and even on horse-drawn buggies. The huge support for the bus boycott was a wake-up call. Black Montgomery citizens were ready to unite and take action.

Rosa Parks heads into the Montgomery courthouse for her trial in March 1956. In 1992, Parks published *Rosa Parks: My Story*, an autobiography about her life in the South and her role in the Montgomery bus boycott.

While the boycott was taking place, Rosa Parks was due in court. Hundreds of African Americans gathered outside Montgomery's city hall, where Parks was being tried. Judge John Scott pronounced Parks guilty of disorderly conduct and violation of Montgomery's segregation laws. He ordered her to pay a $10 fine and $4 in court costs. Parks's attorney, Fred Gray, immediately proclaimed that his client would **appeal** the judge's decision. Parks's appeal would be the first step to challenge the legality of Alabama's segregation laws.

After the trial, leaders discussed extending the boycott. The Montgomery Improvement Association (MIA) was formed to oversee the plan. A list of demands for the bus company included the hiring of Black drivers, courteous treatment of Black riders by white drivers, and a modified seating plan. The modest list did not seek desegregation: the boycotters simply wanted to secure improved riding conditions.

Black women make their way to work on foot during the Montgomery bus boycott.

Dozens of Montgomery's Black leaders, including ministers and prominent business people, were present for the meeting at the Mount Zion AME Church to discuss support for an extended boycott. The attendees voted Dr. King as the first president of the newly formed MIA. King was new to the city and did not have as many enemies as the other leaders. His new position made the 26-year-old minister the key figure associated with the bus boycott.

Though the leaders of the Black community had agreed to continue the boycott, it remained uncertain whether the protest would continue. The boycott required the commitment of Montgomery's African

American bus riders. They would have to agree to avoid riding the buses for the length of the boycott. A meeting was called for later that night at the Holt Street Baptist Church to determine if the Black community would support the idea.

Hundreds of African Americans crowded into the church that night. A loudspeaker system was set up outside for the 4,000 others who gathered to hear the proceedings inside. Speaking in his new role as president of the MIA, King inspired the audience. "We're tired of being segregated and humiliated," he said. "Tired of being kicked about by the brutal feet of oppression." This was King's first great public speech on the road to becoming America's greatest civil rights leader. The vote at the end of the meeting was **unanimous**: the Black citizens of Montgomery voted to continue the boycott.

Dr. King speaking to members of the Montgomery Improvement Association.

The Challenges Mount

The boycott continued through December. To get people to and from work, the MIA established a car pool system that included more than 200 vehicles. Riders gathered at several main hubs where they were picked up by volunteer drivers and taken to their destinations.

As the days wore on, the protest took a terrible toll on the boycotters. The long hours of working the car pool placed physical demands on the drivers. The MIA, which paid the gas bills, had to continually collect money at its weekly meetings with Montgomery's Black residents. Many boycotters were unable to get to their places of work regularly, or on time. Some lost their jobs.

A group of African Americans get into an automobile to carpool during the bus boycott. An empty Montgomery City Lines bus is seen in the background.

Boycotters walk to work rather than ride the bus. "It is more honorable to walk in dignity than ride in humiliation," said Dr. King.

City officials **harassed** the boycotters. Police officers ticketed and jailed car pool drivers for phony violations, such as driving too slowly. African Americans who gathered at car pool hubs were arrested for **loitering**. Police targeted taxi drivers, hoping to prevent them from carrying boycotting passengers. Rather than break the boycotters' will to press on, however, the city's continued harassment strengthened the protesters' commitment. They did not waver in their quest for fair and equal treatment.

A Crippling Effect

The boycott soon had a significant economic impact on the bus company, Montgomery City Lines, and local merchants. The company was losing more than $3,000 a day, while Christmas sales at downtown stores shrank severely. Many Black citizens donated their saved holiday money to support the activities of the MIA. Merchants were dealt another blow when the bus company canceled all city bus service from December 22 through December 25. To make up for lost revenue due to the loss of Black ridership, the bus company had to raise its fare, which in turn reduced white ridership.

Nevertheless, city officials refused to **negotiate** a compromise with the boycotters. As the new year rolled around, boycotters and city officials were locked in a tense stalemate. ■

An Integrated Championship

On October 4, 1955, the Brooklyn Dodgers defeated the New York Yankees in Game Seven of the World Series to win their first and only world championship. The Dodgers team featured six African Americans, including Jackie Robinson.

In 1947, the Brooklyn Dodgers became the first major league baseball team to integrate. On April 15, Jackie Robinson stepped onto Ebbets Field in Brooklyn to become the first African American player in Major League Baseball. In the following years, the Dodgers led the integration of baseball, signing other standout Black players, including pitchers Don Newcombe and Joe Black, catcher Roy Campanella, and infielder Jim Gilliam.

In 1962, Jackie Robinson became the first African American ballplayer to be inducted into the National Baseball Hall of Fame.

Dr. King's home was bombed while he spoke at a church meeting. Here he addresses a crowd from his front porch after the bombing, urging his followers not to react with violence.

The Legacy of 1955 in Civil Rights History

Many white residents in Montgomery, including city officials, grew increasingly angry with the African American boycotters and their leaders. It was only a matter of time before violence erupted.

Targeting the Leaders

On January 30, 1956, someone threw a bomb onto the front porch of the Montgomery home of Dr. King. The explosion tore a large hole in the concrete floor of the porch and blew out windows in the front of the house. No one was harmed, and King held to his commitment of nonviolence. "Don't do anything panicky at all," he told his followers. "This movement will not stop, for what we are doing is just."

Three days later, on February 2, a bomb was tossed onto the front porch of E. D. Nixon's house. The bomb rolled off the porch and exploded when it landed on the ground. No one was injured.

Rosa Parks rides on a newly integrated bus following the Supreme Court decision that ended the Montgomery bus boycott.

The Boycott Ends

On February 1, 1956, attorney Fred Gray—with support from the MIA and the NAACP—filed a lawsuit on behalf of five Black citizens who were arrested on Montgomery buses for violating city segregation laws. Among the plaintiffs were Claudette Colvin, Mary Louise Smith, and Aurelia Browder, who had been arrested on a bus in April 1955. The lawsuit challenged the legality of the state law that allowed segregation on public transportation.

On May 11, a three-judge panel in a federal court heard arguments in the case *Browder v. Gayle*. The panel ruled that segregated seating was unconstitutional. Montgomery city officials immediately appealed the ruling to the U.S. Supreme Court for review. Meanwhile, the bus boycott continued.

On November 13, 1956, the Supreme Court upheld the lower court's decision in *Browder v. Gayle*. The ruling ended racial segregation on public transportation in Alabama.

The Montgomery bus boycott officially ended on December 20, 1956, after 381 days. The next day, Montgomery City Lines resumed full service on all its routes—and all the buses were integrated. This would be just one step in the journey toward equality for Black Americans. The years following would see more upheaval as activists built upon the changes of 1955. ■

A group of African Americans boards an integrated bus through the once-prohibited front door. The Alabama State Capitol is seen in the background.

WASHINGTON PARK

Buy! Daily Producers EGG NOG

2856

Maxine Waters

Many people consider Congresswoman Maxine Waters one of the most powerful women in American politics today.

However, her success was not guaranteed, despite her hard work and ambition. Without the work of civil rights activists that began in 1955, Waters might never have succeeded in public office, where she has served for more than 40 years. During that time, she has emerged as an effective advocate for the rights of people of color, women, children, and the poor.

Representative Maxine Waters, chair of the House Financial Services Committee, listens during a hearing in Washington, DC, in February 2020.

Waters was born in 1938 in St. Louis, Missouri, the fifth of 13 children raised by her single mother. After she graduated from high school, the family moved to Los Angeles, California. There, Waters became an assistant teacher and coordinator with the Head Start program in the **low-income** Watts neighborhood. Head Start is a federal education program designed to meet the needs of low-income children and their families.

After serving as chief deputy to a city council member in 1973, Waters was elected to the California State Assembly in 1976. While in the

Assembly, Waters was a sharp critic of apartheid, the system of racial segregation that existed in South Africa. She was also responsible for legislation that required state agencies to award public-works contracts to minorities and women. Waters authored tenants' rights laws and is responsible for legislation protecting children from abuse.

Representative Waters in 1995.

"I want our millennials and our young people to do what they started out doing with meet-ups— to talk about what is going on, and spread the education."

—MAXINE WATERS

After serving for 14 years in the California State Assembly, Waters was elected to the U.S. House of Representatives for California's 29th congressional district in 1990. In November 2018, she was elected to her 15th term in the House, still serving the district whose individual and family income is below the national average. During her years of service, Waters became the first woman and the first African American to chair the House Financial Services Committee. She is also a member and past chair of the Congressional Black Caucus.

Waters, then president of the Congressional Black Caucus, speaks for Haitian immigrants in 1997.

A prominent leader of the Democratic Party, Waters authored legislation that provides grants to states and local governments to restore poor and abandoned neighborhoods.

Waters has earned a reputation as an outspoken and tough politician. She has sharply criticized both Republican and Democratic presidents, including Barack Obama, whom she accused of not having done enough to help Black Americans. In 2019 and 2020, Waters voted for the impeachment of President Donald Trump. In December 2020, as chair of the House Financial Services Committee, Waters worked to secure billions of dollars in aid for individuals, families, and businesses affected by the COVID-19 virus.

TIMELINE

The Year in Civil Rights

1955

JANUARY 7

Marian Anderson becomes the first African American soloist to sing at New York's Metropolitan Opera House.

MARCH 2

High school student Claudette Colvin is arrested for refusing to give up her seat on a bus in Montgomery, Alabama.

APRIL 5

Mississippi passes a law penalizing white students with jail and fines for attending school with Black students.

MAY 31

In *Brown II*, the Supreme Court orders that desegregation cited in its *Brown v. Board of Education* (1954) ruling must occur with "with all deliberate speed."

JUNE 29

A federal judge rules that African Americans cannot be refused admission to the University of Alabama because of their race.

JULY 14

A federal court rules that desegregation on Columbia, South Carolina, buses is illegal.

JULY 17

Disneyland opens in Anaheim, California, but is inaccessible to most Black people.

AUGUST 1

Georgia's board of education fires all Black teachers who are members of the NAACP.

AUGUST 28

Fourteen-year-old Emmett Till from Chicago is kidnapped and murdered in Money, Mississippi.

OCTOBER 22

Sixteen-year-old John Earl Reese is killed in Gregg County, Texas.

NOVEMBER 7

The Interstate Commerce Commission bans racial segregation on trains and buses in interstate travel.

DECEMBER 1

Rosa Parks is arrested and jailed for refusing to give up her seat on a Montgomery City Lines bus.

DECEMBER 5

The NAACP and citizens of Montgomery begin the Montgomery bus boycott.

GLOSSARY

abolitionist (ab-uh-LISH-uh-nist) someone who worked to abolish slavery before the Civil War

acquittal (uh-KWIT-uhl) a not-guilty verdict

activist (AK-tiv-ist) a person who works to bring about political or social change

alienate (ALE-ee-uhn-ayt) to make a person or group unfriendly, especially one that was formerly supportive

apartheid (uh-PAAR-tide) in South Africa, a policy and system of segregation and discrimination on grounds of race

appeal (uh-PEEL) an application to a higher court for a change in a legal decision

boycott (BOI-kaht) a refusal to buy something or do business with someone as a protest

catalyst (KAT-uh-list) a person or thing that causes something to happen

civil disobedience (SIV-uhl dis-uh-BEE-dee-uhnce) the refusal to observe certain laws, as a peaceful form of protest

civil rights (SIV-uhl rites) the individual rights that all members of a democratic society have to freedom and equal treatment under the law

desegregate (dee-SEG-ruh-gayt) to do away with the practice of separating people of different races in schools, restaurants, and other public places

discrimination (dis-krim-uh-NAY-shuhn) prejudice or unfair behavior to others based on differences in such things as race, gender, or age

exhume (egz-YOOM) to dig a corpse, or dead body, out of the ground

expel (ek-SPEL) to force someone to leave a school or organization

federal (FED-ur-uhl) national government, as opposed to state or local government

harass (huh-RAS) to bother or annoy someone again and again

integrate (IN-tuh-grayt) to include people of all races

Jim Crow (jim kro) the former practice of segregating Black people in the United States

legislature (LEJ-uhs-lay-chur) a group of people who have the power to make or change laws for a country or state

loiter (LOY-tur) to stand around aimlessly or move slowly with many stops

low-income (loh IN-kuhm) when a person or family earns or receives a small amount of money, especially from working

lynching (LIN-ching) a sometimes public murder by a group of people, often involving hanging

negotiate (ni-GOH-shee-ayt) to try to reach an agreement by discussing something or making a bargain

nonviolent resistance (non-VYE-uh-luhnt ri-ZIS-tuhnce) peaceful demonstration for political purpose

oppression (uh-PRESH-uhn) the act of treating people in a cruel and unjust way

segregation (seg-ruh-GAY-shuhn) the act or practice of keeping people or groups apart

sit-in (SIT-in) a form of protest in which demonstrators occupy a place, refusing to leave until their demands are met

unanimous (yoo-NAN-uh-muhs) agreed on by everyone

unconstitutional (uhn-kahn-stuh-TOO-shuh-nuhl) not in keeping with the basic principles or laws set forth in the U.S. Constitution

BIBLIOGRAPHY

Brinkley, Douglas. *Rosa Parks: A Life.* New York: Penguin Books, 2005.

Crowe, Chris. *Getting Away With Murder: The True Story of the Emmett Till Case.* New York: Phyllis Fogelman Books, 2003.

Gorn, Elliott J. *Let the People See: The Story of Emmett Till.* New York: Oxford University Press, 2018.

Lebron, Christopher, J. *The Making of Black Lives Matter.* New York: Oxford University Press, 2017.

The Montgomery Bus Boycott and the Women Who Started It. The Memoir of Jo Ann Gibson Robinson. University of Tennessee Press, 1987.

Morris, Aldon D. *The Origins of the Civil Rights Movement: Black Communities Organizing for Change.* New York: Free Press, 1984.

Packard, Jerrold M. *American Nightmare: The History of Jim Crow.* New York: St. Martin's Press, 2002.

Rothstein, Richard. *The Color of Law: A Forgotten History of How Our Government Segregated America.* New York: Liveright, 2017.

Tyson, Timothy B. *The Blood of Emmett Till.* New York: Simon & Schuster, 2017.

Whitfield, Stephen J. *A Death in the Delta: The Story of Emmett Till*. Baltimore: Johns Hopkins University Press, 1988.

Williams, Donnie, with Wayne Greenhaw. *The Thunder of Angels: The Montgomery Bus Boycott and the People Who Broke the Back of Jim Crow*. Chicago: Lawrence Hill Books, 2005.

Workers at the NAACP offices in New York City during a voter registration drive.

biography.com/news/
   martin-luther-king-jr-gandhi-nonviolence-inspiration

history.com/this-day-in-history/
   marian-anderson-sings-on-the-steps-of-the-lincoln-memorial

history.com/this-day-in-history/the-death-of-emmett-till

https://www.naacpldf.org/brown-vs-board/

INDEX

Note: Page numbers in *italics* refer to images and captions.

About the Author

Nel Yomtov is an award-winning author of nonfiction books and graphic novels about American and world history, geography, sports, science, mythology, and military history. He has written numerous titles in Scholastic's True Books, Enchantment of the World, Cornerstones of Freedom, and Calling All Innovators series. Nel lives in the New York City area with his wife, Nancy, an educator. His son, Jess, is a sports journalist and website producer.

PHOTO CREDITS